Who Are The Biblical Israelites?

Benayah Israel

Contents

Who Are The Biblical Israelites?

Benayah Israel

Introduction

During a recent interview, political commentator Tucker Carlson leaned forward and asked Senator Ted Cruz a pointed, even dangerous, question: **"The nation of Israel mentioned in Genesis... is that the same Israel run by Benjamin Netanyahu today?"**

That single question cracks open centuries of silence, dogma, and revision. Because if the answer is no—if today's modern state of Israel is not a direct continuation of the biblical one— then we are forced to confront an uncomfortable reality: **Who, then, were the real Israelites? And where are their descendants today?**

Chapter 1

Who Were the Biblical Israelites?

In roughly 701 BCE, something extraordinary was carved in stone—and it may hold the answer to a question that still stirs controversy today. To investigate this mystery, we follow a trail that leads us not to abstract theology, but to stone walls, scorched ruins, and skeletal remains buried beneath the dust of a ruined city—Lachish.

Figure 1.1. The Lachish Ruins.

In the heart of the ancient kingdom of Judah, during a devastating siege, something rare happened: an Assyrian king commissioned a visual record of his conquest. His name was Sennacherib. His army laid waste to Lachish. And his artists captured, in stunning detail, what the people of Judah looked like at that moment in history.

This archaeological record, known as the Lachish Relief, still survives today. Etched into slabs of gypsum and once mounted in the royal palace at Nineveh, it offers more than a war story. It provides a face. Faces. Dozens of them. Clear, detailed profiles of the people known in the Bible as the "children of Israel."

In the chapters that follow, we don't just explore what the relief shows. We put it under forensic scrutiny. We compare its visual data with the bones recovered from the site. We examine 20th-century cranial measurements, ancient hairstyles, and overlooked 19th-century testimony. We contrast the biological traits of those Judahite skulls with those of modern Jewish and African American populations. And we ask the question most scholars have tiptoed around for decades:

Were the Israelites African in appearance? And if so... why was that story buried?

What follows is not speculation. It is a case file—a historical dossier built from art, archaeology, and anthropological science.

And once the evidence is laid out, the conclusions will speak for themselves.

Chapter 2

Historical Background: Judah, Assyria, and the Siege of Lachish (701 BCE)

The late 8th century BCE was a time of dread across the ancient Near East. Storm clouds gathered over Judah not metaphorical ones, but marching armies, siege towers, and iron chariots.

Judah, the southern Israelite kingdom with its capital in Jerusalem, had made a bold move. Its king, Hezekiah, defied the might of Assyria—then the most fearsome empire on earth. It was an act of rebellion that would trigger an overwhelming response. In 701 BCE, Sennacherib, the brutal monarch of Assyria, unleashed a campaign designed not only to punish— **but to make an example.**

The Biblical account of this attack is very simple. 2 Kings 18:13 New International Version states, *"In the fourteenth year of King Hezekiah's reign, Sennacherib attacked all the fortified cities of Judah and captured them."* But behind that verse is a scene of mass destruction. Sennacherib himself boasted of conquering 46 strongholds and deporting over 200,000 people. The spearhead of that assault was aimed at one critical target: the heavily fortified city of Lachish.

Figure 2.1. Sennacherib's Attack on Lachish, AI generated art, 8 Aug. 2025.

Lachish wasn't just any outpost. It was Judah's second city—its military garrison and shield. If Jerusalem was the heart, Lachish was the iron wall guarding it. Its fall would signal the collapse of Judah's defenses. And so, Sennacherib focused his full military force on it.

The siege that followed was brutal. The Assyrians built an enormous siege ramp, dragging battering rams up against the city's walls. Archers and slingers bombarded from a distance. Fire consumed rooftops. The defenders—likely including Hezekiah's elite guard—fought back with arrows and stones, knowing full well that surrender meant torture, death, or slavery.

Archaeological excavations at Lachish confirm the violence. A destruction layer, Level III, shows the city consumed by fire. Arrowheads litter the site. The remains of the siege ramp still scar the landscape today. This was not just a battle—it was **a total conquest.**

Jerusalem was spared, barely, but Lachish was obliterated. It became the crown jewel of Sennacherib's campaign, the moment he chose to immortalize—not in writing, but in imagery. What he couldn't do in Jerusalem, he made up for by etching his triumph into stone. And so, the Lachish Relief was born.

Chapter 3

Sennacherib's Lachish Relief: Creation and Purpose

Question: What does a victorious tyrant do when he wants the world to remember his wrath?

Answer: He carves it into stone.

Shortly after his brutal siege of Lachish, King Sennacherib of Assyria ordered something unprecedented: a massive, sprawling stone mural to record the conquest in detail. Not in poetic epics. Not in fragile scrolls. But in cold, hard gypsum—**a visual boast meant to outlast empires.**

Figure 3.1. Photograph by Alamy, The Capture of Lachish, Jan. 2015.

This was no minor decoration. The Lachish Relief, as it's now called, once covered the walls of a grand hall in Sennacherib's "South-West Palace" at Nineveh—modern-day Iraq. Measuring over 18 meters long (59.0551 feet) and 2.5 meters high (8.2021 feet), the relief wrapped around an entire chamber like a cinematic storyboard. It told only one story: how Judah's mighty fortress of Lachish fell to the sword and flames of Assyria.

Figure 3.2. Photograph by Alamy, Sennacherib, on a throne, watches as prisoners are brought before him and sometimes executed, about 700-692 BC.

And in case anyone missed the message, Sennacherib spelled it out in cuneiform:

"Sennacherib, the mighty king, king of Assyria, sitting on the throne of judgment, before the city of Lachish (Lakhisha). I give permission for its slaughter."

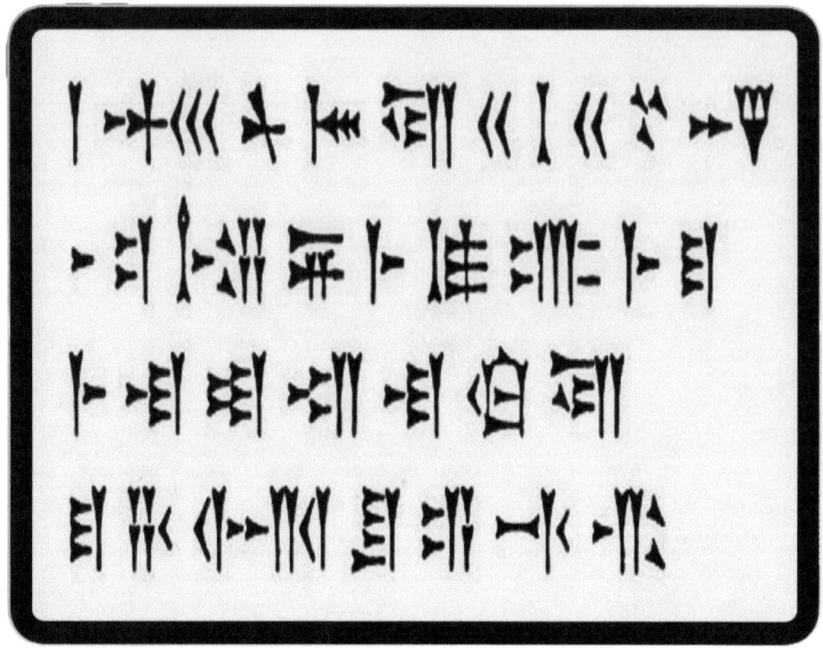

Figure 3.3. Photograph by Almay, Cuneiform inscription from Lachish Relief.

There is no ambiguity here. The king isn't just watching—he's commanding. He is the judge and executioner. He's also—the historian of his violent acts. The imagery was designed to **terrify** those who saw it: enemy envoys, foreign visitors, rebellious vassals. And it was meant to erase the sting of failure—**for while Sennacherib never conquered Jerusalem, he had annihilated Lachish.**

Question: Why this city?

Answer: Because Lachish was Judah's backbone. And because its destruction was complete.

The relief, now housed in the British Museum, is more than imperial art. It's a political weapon. But paradoxically, it also became a priceless archaeological time capsule. For in glorifying his conquest, Sennacherib unintentionally preserved something he had no interest in promoting: **the actual appearance of the people of Judah.**

Figure 3.4. Photography by Almay, Scene from the Lachish Relief depicting the defeated tribe of Judah begging for their lives, 7th Cent. B.C.

Chapter 4

The Siege in Stone: Scenes and Details of the Lachish Relief

Question: What happens when an empire records its violence in stone?

Answer: You get a crime scene frozen in time.

The Lachish Relief is more than artwork—**it's a frame-by-frame breakdown of a siege, rendered with almost obsessive detail.** Like an ancient storyboard, it marches us through the brutal choreography of war: the approach, the assault, the collapse... and the human cost.

Across the stone panels, Assyrian soldiers launch a full-scale assault. Siege engines grind forward. Archers let fly volleys of arrows. Slingers hurl stones.

Figure 4.1. Photograph by Alamy, A detail of an ancient Assyrian stone panel carving (700-692 BC) showing archers attacking the town of Lachish near Jerusalem.

A massive earthen ramp rises against Lachish's walls, and battering rams crash into the city gates. The defenders—cornered, desperate—rain projectiles from the parapets. Fire spreads. Walls crumble.

Figure 4.2. A stone-carved relief depicting an attack on Lachish, Assyria, 700-692 BC.

And then—silence. In the aftermath, we don't just see conquest. We see **suffering**.

The relief shifts focus to the captives. Lines of men, women, and children—residents of Judah—are marched out of their fallen city under armed guard. Some lift their hands in surrender. Others weep. Their faces are carved in expressive detail, their heads bowed, their bodies stooped. This is not triumph. It's trauma, immortalized by the very hands that caused it.

Figure 4.3. Photograph by Almay, Scene from the Lachish Relief depicting the defeated inhabitants begging for their lives, 7th Cent. B.C.

And then **it gets darker.**

In the center panel, Sennacherib sits beneath an ornate canopy, enthroned like a god-judge. He's carved larger than any other figure—**a psychological trick used in ancient art to inflate power.** Kneeling before him are Judean prisoners—men with beards, short woolly hair, and robes torn from battle.

Some plead...

Figure 4.4. The Fall of Lachish: King Sennacherib reviews Judaean prisoners.

Some are punished...

—Two are shown being flayed alive.

Figure 4.5. Photograph by Almay, Stone carved relief depicting prisoners

They were captured after the attack on Lachish, Assyria, about 700-692 BC.

—Another is stabbed as an Assyrian soldier holds him down by the hair.

Figure 4.6. Assyrian soldier, using a dagger, about to behead a prisoner from the city of Lachish, 700-692 BCE.

This isn't a metaphor. It's documentation.

And yet, through the horror, the relief gives us something unexpected: **an ethnographic profile.** A snapshot of what the people of Judah looked like in 701 BCE. Their hair is short, rounded, and woolly—distinct from the long, styled hair of their Assyrian captors. Their garments are simple. Their posture is humble, but their features are unmistakable: broad noses, tightly curled woolly hair, and short-cropped beards.

They were not imagined figures. **They were observed subjects.** and though Sennacherib's sculptors meant to glorify one empire, they may have unintentionally preserved the truth of another: the appearance of the biblical Israelites.

Figure 4.7. The captives are brought before King Sennacherib.

Chapter 5

Echoes in Stone: Nubians at Persepolis and Judah at Lachish

Question: Can a hairstyle carved in stone link distant peoples across empires?

Answer: In the ancient world, it could—and it did.

The **Lachish Relief** we explored in the previous chapter is more than a snapshot of war, it's an ethnographic time-capsule. Amid the chaos of siege and surrender, the Assyrian artists captured telling details of the Judean appearance. We see it in panel after panel: the Judean men under Assyrian guard have **short, rounded, woolly hair**, utterly distinct from the long, flowing locks of their Assyrian captors. These prisoners are not generic figures; they are carved from observation, with tightly curled **"close-cropped" hair and beards** that set them apart. Their features—broad noses, full lips, and coarse hair texture—form a profile that the stone preserves with almost forensic precision. Sennacherib's sculptors, likely without realizing it, created a **visual police lineup** of Judah's people in 701 B.C.E., encoding physical traits for posterity. But was this portrayal unique to Assyrian art? Or were the Judeans being depicted with an established visual code used for other peoples? To answer that, we must look beyond Lachish—to the banks of the Nile, the palaces of Persepolis, and the art of classical Greece and Rome.

Detail of the Lachish relief from Sennacherib's palace (c. 700 B.C.E.). Judean captives (left) kneel in submission before the Assyrian king (far right, on throne). Notice the Judean men's hair: **short, tightly coiled "woolly" curls***, depicted as over fifty small, raised knobs on their scalps, with equally short, curled beards. This hairstyle contrasts with the Assyrian officials who wear longer, stylized hair and longer beards. The Lachish sculptors meticulously differentiated the Judeans by their*

Figure 5.1. The captives are brought before King Sennacherib.

African-type hair texture, *a detail as informative as it is striking.*

A Persian Parallel: Nubians on the Apadana

Over 150 years after Lachish, and some **1,500 miles to the east**, another empire carved a grand scene into stone. In the audience hall of **Persepolis** (the Achaemenid Persian capital), a relief on the Apadana's East Stairs depicts delegations of subject nations bringing tribute to the Persian king. Among them, one group stands out immediately to the eye: the men of **Nubia (Kush)** from Africa's Upper Nile.

Figure 5.2. The captives are brought before King Sennacherib.

Their appearance on this Persian monument is a mirror echo of the Judeans at Lachish. The Nubian tribute bearers are depicted with the same distinctive **short, tightly coiled hairstyle** – a field of raised, round curls covering the scalp. The Persian sculptors painstakingly chiseled around *eighty small knob-like curls* on each Nubian head to capture the texture of **tightly curled woolly hair**. This was no artistic accident or flourish. In ancient sculpture, this "peppercorn" hair technique was a well-known convention used specifically to portray peoples of African heritage.

Figure 5.3 Ethiopians.

What makes the Persepolis scene so compelling is how directly it **parallels the Lachish Relief**. In the Lachish panels, every Judean prisoner, young or old, high or low, wears the same short, woolly hair style rendered in dozens of stone curls. All Judean men at Lachish are shown with neatly woolly beards, and their scalp hair remains the same tight coils, cropped close to the head.

Figure 5.4 AI Image.

At Persepolis, the Nubian envoys appear **clean-shaven (beardless)**, but this only makes the texture of their hair all the more prominent: a crown of dense, curly bumps across each scalp. Separated by two centuries and the vast expanse of the Near East, the Judeans of Assyrian Palestine and the Nubians of Persian Iran are depicted with **identical hairstyles**. The implication is as bold as it is unmistakable: across cultures and empires, artists used the *same* iconographic language to represent a certain ethnic reality – namely, a people with **short, tightly coiled, "African" hair**.

This is not an artistic coincidence or a case of two sculptors independently inventing the same idea. It appears to be a deliberate visual code, a sculptural shorthand by which ancient empires marked out the appearance of African peoples in their art.

Figure 5.5 Moors.

The Assyrians who carved Lachish and the Persians who carved Persepolis lived in different worlds, spoke different languages, and conquered different peoples – yet both chose nearly identical methods to render the hair of these subjects. In essence, **the Judeans of Lachish were depicted using the same**

hairstyle conventions that an Egyptian or Persian artist would use to depict Nubians or Ethiopians. The artistic message is clear without a single written word: *these people look like those people.* Little wonder then that the reliefs confirm a truth that later ages would forget – that the biblical Israelites of Judah were, in physical appearance, akin to the Africans to their south. The conquerors' chisels affirmed what text alone might obscure.

Side-by-Side: Persepolis vs. Lachish

- **Persepolis (Apadana East Stairs – Nubian Delegation):** The Nubian tribute bearers are shown bare-headed and clean-shaven. Their hair is rendered as a multitude of **small, rounded bumps** (about 80 across the scalp) each bump meticulously carved to represent a tight coil of hair. The curls are evenly distributed and rise off the head in clear relief, a technique long used to signify the **coarse, woolly hair** of African peoples.
- **Lachish (Assyrian Palace Relief – Siege of Judah):** The Judean captives are shown under armed guard, some kneeling or prostrate. Like the Nubians, they wear their hair **short and woolly**, indicated by rows of **pebble-like curls** cut into the stone. On some figures, one can count **dozens of tightly curled hairs** covering

the scalp. Judean men sport short curly beards as well, but notably **no long tresses** – their hair is cropped close in the same manner as the Nubian delegation.

- **The Match:** Both reliefs — created by different empires and for different purposes — employ an identical visual vocabulary to characterize these subjects. In each case, **small, raised coils** are used to depict tightly coiled African-style hair. At Persepolis, this feature identifies tribute-bearers from Nubia; at Lachish, it marks the people of Judah. The consistency is striking: artists in both Mesopotamian and Persian spheres clearly associated this short, kinky hair texture with the people they were portraying. It's a cross-confirmation in stone that **the men of Judah were carved with the same hair texture as Africans**.

Earlier Echoes: Nubians in Egyptian Art

This artistic convention of portraying Africans with **woolly hair** did not begin in Assyria or Persia. Centuries before Sennacherib's armies ever approached Judah, the pharaohs of **Egypt** had been in contact and conflict with their southern neighbors in Nubia. Egyptian tombs and temples from the New Kingdom (c. 1500–1100 B.C.E.) are filled with painted and carved scenes of Nubians – as enemies, allies, traders, and tribute bearers. In these scenes, Egyptian artists consistently used the same visual cues to distinguish the Nubians from Egyptians. Foremost among those cues was **hair texture**.

In Egyptian art, Nubian men are typically depicted with **short-cropped, tightly curled hair** or sometimes wearing **short "Nubian wigs"** that emulate that curled style.

Figure 5.6 Nubians wearing hair wigs.

Their hair is often painted dark and shown as a cap of small ringlets or clumps. A vivid example comes from the tomb of Horemheb (c. 1320 B.C.E.): a relief from his Saqqara tomb shows a line of captured Nubian prisoners with unmistakably African features – dark skin, broad noses, and tightly curled hair rendered in low-relief curls. They sit on the ground, hands bound, under the watch of Egyptian guards. The sculptor distinguished their hair by carving textured, clumped curls, in contrast to the straight or wavy hair used for prisoners in other scenes. An inscription even records that a scribe is selecting two of these Nubian captives for royal service – evidence that their appearance was noteworthy enough to record in detail.

Faience tiles depicting bound Nubian prisoners from the mortuary temple of Pharaoh Ramesses III at Medinet Habu (c. 1180 B.C.E.).

Figure 5.7 Nubians.

These glazed tiles, each about the size of a hand, show Nubian men with classic African features: **dark brown skin, oval faces, and tightly curled black hair**. Note how the artist indicated the **short, woolly hair** – the curls are painted as dense, peppercorn-like dots or bumps encircling the head. Each prisoner also wears a characteristic Nubian earring and patterned tunic. Such tiles were inlaid on temple walls or furniture, symbolically "binding" Egypt's enemies. The short curly hairstyle here is the same visual marker later seen at Lachish and Persepolis, underscoring a long continuity in how African peoples were portrayed in the ancient Nile Valley and Near East.

Figure 5.8 Egyptian soldiers and Nubian mercenaries around 1470 BC Deir el-Bahri, the mortuary temple of Queen, Hatshepsut.

Egyptian artists, like the Assyrians and Persians after them, clearly **recognized the unique hair texture of Nilotic African peoples** and made it a hallmark of their depiction. Whether in battle scenes showing Pharaoh triumphing over Nubian chiefs, or in peaceful processions of Nubian tribute bearers bringing gold, ivory, and exotic animals, the Nubians are almost invariably shown with short, **kinky hair**. Sometimes the Nubian men sport a distinctive conical headpiece or a headband with a feather, but even then the sculptor will show the texture of the hair at the sides – tight curls peeking out. The Egyptians even developed a fashionable wig style in their own society called the "Nubian wig," imitating the short, round curly look of Nubian hair. In other words, this hair texture was so closely associated with Nubians that it became part of the Egyptian visual repertoire both in art and in elite fashion.

By the time the Assyrians carved Lachish, the image of **"a man with short, tightly curled hair"** as a stereotyped African was already at least 500 years old. The Assyrian reliefs simply carried that stereotype into Mesopotamia. When we set the Lachish panels beside Egyptian tomb paintings, the **continuity is striking**. A Nubian soldier in a Deir el-Bahri mortuary of Queen, Hatshepsut around 1470 B.C.E. has the same cropped curly hair (painted black, in tiny ringlets) that a Judean prisoner is carved with in 700 B.C.E. on a palace wall in Nineveh.

Different empires, different eras, yet the visual shorthand remained. This strengthens the conclusion that the Lachish artists were faithfully rendering an ethnic reality the ancient world understood: the people of Judah, like other peoples of African-descent or African-admixture, had hair that grew in **tightly coiled, woolly curls** rather than in loose waves or straight locks.

Later Echoes: Africans in Greco-Roman Art

The use of raised curls to denote African hair did not end with the Persian Empire. The succeeding eras—Greek, Hellenistic, and Roman—continued to depict Africans in sculpture and art with the same attentive emphasis on hair texture. In fact, some of the most lifelike portrayals of African individuals in antiquity come from the Greco-Roman world, where artists sculpted in marble and bronze with astounding realism. Once again, we find those **short, tight curls** immortalized in stone.

A compelling example is a marble head commonly titled **"Head of a Man with Tight, Curly Hair,"** dated to the late 2nd century B.C.E. (Ptolemaic period). Discovered in the Eastern Mediterranean and now in the Brooklyn Museum, this sculpture is a portrait of what appears to be a Nubian or other sub-Saharan African man rendered in a Hellenistic Greek style.

The man's face is powerfully modeled: broad nose, full lips, and deep-set eyes, all features that suggest an African identity. But it is the hair that truly captivates the viewer.

Figure 5.9 Nubian.

The sculptor carved the hair in countless **small spiral locks** that cover the scalp in a dense cluster of twists and curls. Each curl is **drilled and chiseled in three dimensions**, protruding from the head in knotted loops of stone. The result is that even in monochrome marble, one instantly recognizes the texture of coarse, kinky hair. It is a masterwork of realism and cultural representation – the artist has **captured the tight coil of African hair with meticulous skill**.

Greco-Roman art provides many other instances. On Roman mosaics and frescoes, for example, Ethiopian hunters or servants are often shown with short curly hair in contrast to the straight or wavy hair of Europeans. On painted Greek vases, figures identified as Ethiopians (Aithiopes) are typically given very dark complexions and curly hair rendered by black dotting or tight spiral brushstrokes. Roman sculptors created bronzes of African boys and men (sometimes as lampstands or decorative figures) with extraordinarily lifelike curly hairstyles. The message carried through: **hair was a key ethnic signifier**. A Roman viewer could distinguish an "Ethiopian" figure at a glance by the hair alone.

What is fascinating is that despite the changing aesthetics from Egyptian to Assyrian to Greek art, *the portrayal of African hair remains consistent*. This consistent portrayal across time and culture suggests that the underlying **physical reality** was consistent as well. Simply put, artists were observing real people of African heritage and recording their traits in the visual medium of their day. Those tightly curled hairstyles on ancient walls and statues are reflections of real hairstyles and hair textures worn by real people. And those real people – be they Nubians, Ethiopians, or Judeans – evidently shared a physical trait of **African-Asiatic type hair** that set them apart from Persian, or European populations around them.

Figure 5.10 Terracotta vase in the form of a black African youth's head Classical 4th century BC Etruscan 23cm Etruria Italy.

A Visual Testimony Across Empires

When we line up these findings, an elegant truth reveals itself. The short, woolly hair carved on the heads of Judah's captives at Lachish was not an isolated artistic quirk, but part of a **long-standing visual tradition**. Egyptian pharaohs, Assyrian kings, Persian emperors, and Roman patricians all instructed their artists to portray the world as they saw it – and when it came to portraying the peoples of Africa (or those seen as related to Africa), they all gravitated to the *same* defining feature: **hair texture**. The consistency of this feature in art is remarkable. It spans over a millennium of human history and the breadth of the ancient, civilized world. It is as if the stones themselves are speaking, repeating the same description in different languages of art: *these people have tightly curled hair.*

For the modern reader, the import is profound. It means that the Judean Israelites, who lived in the crossroads of Africa and Asia, were depicted by their contemporaries as physically akin to the Africans. Their **ethnicity** was recorded not in writing but in the very way their hair was carved in relief. Ancient conquerors had no political motivation to exaggerate or alter the appearance of these subject peoples – if anything, artists tended to portray foreigners *stereotypically accurately*, to better boast of the empire's conquests over diverse lands. The Lachish artist had likely seen Nubians in Egyptian or Assyrian art (or even in person, given the reach of empires), and when he chiseled the Judeans' hair, he used the same shorthand. In doing so, he and those like him **"carved forever into history"** a confirmation of Judah's identity.

The evidence, gathered from museums and monuments across the world, speaks in unison. In **Lachish and Persepolis**, in **Thebes and Nineveh**, in **Athens and Rome**, the image of the African–the Nubian, the Kushite, the Ethiopian, the Judean–was consistently rendered with short, tightly coiled hair and often darker complexion. It is a chorus of stone voices, an ancient consensus. The Biblical Israelites of Judah, far from the fair-skinned figures of Renaissance imagination, bore the hallmarks of an African-affiliated people: **woolly hair and bronze complexions** among them.

And so, the **short woolly hair of the Judean captives** on the Lachish Relief finds its brothers on the walls of pharaonic tombs and the stairways of Persian palaces. The silent testimony of art aligns with the clues of crania and the whispers of text. A portrait comes into focus: the children of Israel, in their native land, looked much like the children of Cush. The same curls that crown the Nubian's head on the Nile adorn the Judean peasant in the hills of Judah. The past has left us these echoes in stone – we need only look and listen. Each curl carved in relief is a word in the visual language of antiquity, and together they tell a story long obscured: **the Israelites were a people of color, recognized and recorded by the great empires of their day**. The affirmation spans continents and centuries, patiently waiting in museum cases and on temple walls for us to heed it. The ancient artists have spoken. In the enduring medium of stone, they preserved an image of the Biblical Israelites that transcends time and conqueror – an image with hair tightly coiled, proudly short and "woolly," linking the sons of Judah to the sons of Africa in an unbroken cultural memory carved in stone.

Modern Echoes: Bantu Knots, Sponge Curls, and Judahite Hair

Assyrian observers clearly noted this unique look – the relief essentially "marked the Judeans by their short woolly curls," distinguishing them from the long-haired Assyrians. Visually, the Judeans' rounded, sectioned hair clumps bear a striking resemblance to modern Bantu knots and sponge curls, with hair appearing in multiple small coil-like segments. This uncanny parallel suggests that what was a common Judahite hairstyle millennia ago is immediately recognizable to us today in the form of an African-derived style.

Figure 5.11 Sponge curl

Bantu knots, as worn by many Bantu-speaking Africans and African Americans, involve sectioning the hair and twisting it into numerous small coiled buns evenly distributed across the head. The result is a pattern of rounded knots that looks very much like the "peppercorn" textured curls depicted on the Lachish captives. This hairstyle – traced back hundreds of years to the Zulu people (where they are also called Zulu knots) – carries deep cultural meaning.

Figure 5.12 Bantu or Zulu Knots.

For those who wear Bantu knots today, the style is more than just fashion: it is a connection to heritage and identity.

Historically a practical protective style for tightly curled hair, Bantu knots have come to symbolize pride in African ancestry and a celebration of natural hair texture. Beyond the physical similarity in appearance, both the ancient Judahite hair, modern curls, and modern Bantu knots serve as cultural identifiers. In the ancient relief, the Judeans' short, curled hair set them apart ethnically in the eyes of their contemporaries. Likewise, Bantu knots in modern times are often an expression of Black identity and cultural legacy, worn to honor African roots and personal creativity. In both cases, a hairstyle conveys more than style – it tells a story of a people. The parallel between the Lachish relief and contemporary Bantu knots and sponge curls bridges thousands of years, underscoring how hairstyles can endure as a meaningful link between past and present, between an ancient Judean community and the African diaspora today.

Figure 5.13 Sponge Curls.

Chapter 6

The Bloodline of Jacob: The Genetic Signature of Israel

Question: How does a nation trace its bloodline to one man?

Answer: Through the fathers who carried his name, and the sons who carried his seed.

"Your name shall not be called Jacob anymore, but Israel shall be your name." — Genesis 35:10–12

"Gather yourselves together, and hear, ye sons of Jacob; and hearken unto Israel your father... All these are the twelve tribes of Israel: and this is that which their father spake unto them, and blessed them." —Genesis 49:1–2, 28

Jacob's Blessing and the Birth of a Nation

Jacob—renamed Israel—stands at the beginning of a story that merges bloodline and covenant. In him, twelve sons became the framework of an entire people. Each son, born to one of four mothers, carried forward not just a family name but a single paternal signature—the Y-chromosome of their father Jacob. It was the invisible thread binding Israel's tribes together in every generation.

Twelve Sons, Four Mothers, One Bloodline

The genealogical record preserved in Genesis reads like an ancestral chart written in flesh and spirit. Leah bore Reuben, Simeon, Levi, Judah, Issachar, and Zebulun. Rachel bore Joseph and Benjamin. Bilhah, Rachel's handmaid, bore Dan and Naphtali. Zilpah, Leah's handmaid, bore Gad and Asher. Though their mothers differed, all twelve sons shared the same father—Israel—and thus the same paternal DNA.

Figure 6.1. The Family Tree of Jacob (Israel)

Abraham → Isaac → Jacob (Israel)

├── Leah: Reuben, Simeon, Levi, Judah, Issachar, Zebulun

├── Rachel: Joseph, Benjamin

├── Bilhah: Dan, Naphtali

└── Zilpah: Gad, Asher

Uniformity in Stone: Judah at Lachish

Question: What does a shared hairstyle have to do with genetics? Answer: Everything, when that hairstyle reflects a shared inheritance.

The Lachish Relief, carved in Assyrian stone, offers something that ancient scribes never wrote—portraits of the sons of Judah. Each captive shown at Lachish bears the same short, woolly hair and the same broad features. The sculptors captured what words could not: a family resemblance extending from Jacob's tent to Hezekiah's city walls.

The Y-Chromosome of Israel

In biology, the Y-chromosome is a perfect recordkeeper. It is passed only from father to son—unchanged, except for small mutations over centuries. If Jacob's sons lived today, their Y-DNA would still bear the same paternal marker. Each tribe would represent a branch of that single tree. The line of Judah, from which kings and prophets came, carried Jacob's genetic signature—the same line carved into stone at Lachish.

The Haplogroup of a Nation: E1B1A and the African Diaspora

When modern geneticists examine the Y-chromosomes of African American men, they find a startling pattern.

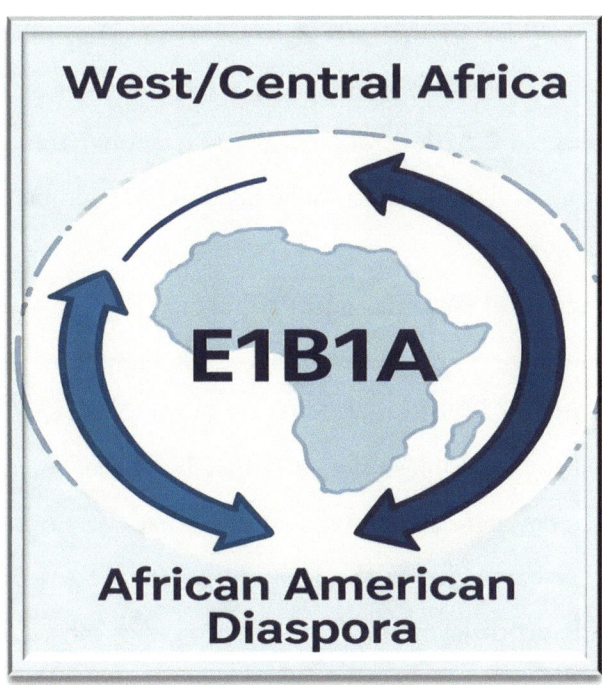

Overwhelmingly, they trace to one lineage: Haplogroup E1B1A. This haplogroup, also known as E-M2, dominates in West and Central Africa—the same regions from which millions were taken in the Transatlantic Slave Trade. Despite the vast diversity of Africa, this one paternal signature appears again and again. It points back to a single ancestral line—a shared father from an ancient time.

Admixture and Historical Trauma

But there's another story written in the genes. A minority of African American Y-chromosomes belong to European haplogroups such as R1b or I. These are not the markers of migration—they are the scars of enslavement. They reflect the violence of the slave trade, when European men forced themselves upon African women. Yet even through this horror, the dominant line—E1B1A—remained. The bloodline of the fathers endured.

The Witness of Genetics and Prophecy

In the language of science, a haplogroup is a mutation pattern. In the language of Scripture, it is a testimony. The genetic data reveal what the prophets declared: that Israel was one family, bound by covenant and blood. A single father—Jacob—passed down his name, his faith, and his genetic code. Though scattered and enslaved, his sons still carry that inheritance in their cells. The Lachish stones preserved their likeness; modern genetics preserves their lineage.

Conclusion: The Restoration of a Forgotten Lineage

The evidence converges—archaeology, Scripture, and science all speak with one voice. The children of Israel were one paternal family. The same Y-chromosome that coursed through Jacob's veins still moves through his sons today. Among the scattered descendants of Africa's diaspora, that lineage endures as Haplogroup E1B1A. It is the silent witness of a covenant unbroken and a prophecy fulfilled. The day has come when Israel remembers itself—not by myth, but by blood, bone, and revelation.

"And they shall remember their own land, which they had polluted... and they shall know that I am the Lord their God."
— Ezekiel 20:42–44

Chapter 7

Clues from the Bones: Cranial Analysis of Lachish Remains

If the relief shows us their faces, the ground tells us the rest of the story.

In the 1930s, archaeologists made a grim discovery beneath the ruins of Lachish. Hidden inside what is now known as Cave 120, they unearthed a mass of human remains—hundreds of skulls and bones, scorched and broken, sealed beneath a layer of ash and destruction.

Figure 5.1. Commander's house, Lachish archaeological site.

Figure 5.2. Main gate, Lachish archaeological site, Israel.

It was the aftermath of Sennacherib's siege, preserved in limestone and dust. But for physical anthropologists, it was also something more: **a biological archive**—an opportunity to study, firsthand, the people who once walked the streets of ancient Judah.

Who were they—genetically, anatomically? Where did they come from? Did they resemble today's Jewish populations? Or did their bones tell a different story?

The first serious answers came in 1939, when British anatomist D.L. Risdon published a landmark study analyzing the Lachish skulls. His findings? Shocking for their time.

Section 1: The Study

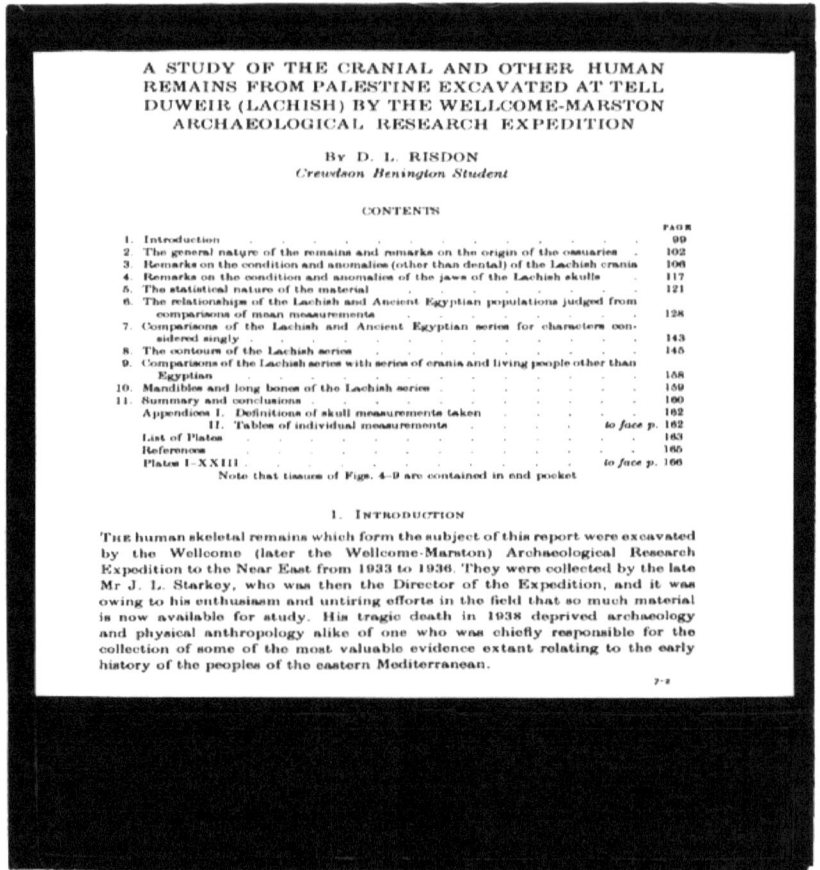

Figure 5.3. D.L. Risdon, Published study of the cranial analysis of Lachish remains, 1939.

The skulls, he concluded, bore "very similar" traits to those of **dynastic Egyptians**—specifically from **Upper Egypt**, the southern Nile Valley. This region, known for its dark-skinned populations with elongated skull shapes, historically overlapped with Nubian and Sudanese groups. Risdon proposed that the people of Lachish may have descended from just such a population: **an Egypto-Nubian group planted deep in the land of Judah.**

Decades later, others returned to the bones. In 1981, anthropologists Musgrave and Evans reviewed the crania and reached the same conclusion: an apparent affinity with Egyptian skeletal types.

But the most rigorous analysis came in 1988. Dr. Shomarka Keita, a Harvard-trained physical anthropologist, applied multivariate statistical techniques to compare the Lachish skulls with crania from across Africa and the Mediterranean. The results were conclusive. The population at Lachish wasn't uniform, but a significant portion **clustered most closely with North African, Egyptian, and Nubian populations.**

Not Canaanites. Not Mesopotamians. Not Greeks. **Africans.**

Keita found that several individual skulls could not be statistically distinguished from Nubians—even when the model allowed them to be identified as "Lachish." The biological overlap with Nile Valley populations was that strong. He summarized it plainly: "The Egypto-Nubian presence is supported."

In other words, the people of Judah—at Lachish—showed unmistakable ties to Northeast Africa. It wasn't just a cultural exchange. It was genetic, skeletal, undeniable.

And if that weren't enough, the shape of their heads told the same story.

Section 2: Skull Shapes and Silent Witnesses: The Cephalic Index

So far, the visual and skeletal evidence suggests a single conclusion: the people of ancient Judah bore a greater resemblance to Egyptians and Nubians than to Europeans. But how do we quantify that? How do we move from visual impression to scientific precision?

Enter the Cephalic Index (CI).

This anthropological tool, developed in the 19th century, measures the ratio of skull width to skull length (breadth ÷ length × 100). The result classifies skulls into three major types:

- **Dolichocephalic** (long-headed): CI under 75

- **Mesocephalic** (medium-headed): CI 75–79.9

- **Brachycephalic** (round-headed): CI 80 and above

While the concept has limitations, it remains a helpful way to track population traits over time.

When British anatomist D.L. Risdon measured the skulls from Lachish, he found something striking: **the Judahites were overwhelmingly dolichocephalic**. The average cephalic index for males was 74.3, and for females, it was 75.5. These are long, narrow skulls—the kind most commonly associated with Northeast African populations, including ancient Egyptians.

By contrast, modern Jewish populations—especially Ashkenazi Jews—have much higher cranial index values. For example, 17th-century Prague Jewish skulls measured by anthropologist J. Matiegka showed an average CI of 82.0, placing them firmly in the round-headed (brachycephalic) range. Even the average for Jewish males in Palestine hovered around 77.9— significantly broader than the Lachish profile.

Here's where it gets even more compelling: 20th-century studies of African American males reveal cephalic index values between **73 and 75 in the Deep South—almost identical** to the Lachish remains.

Region/Group	Average CI	Admixture Level	Source
Rural Alabama/Georgia African Americans	~74	Low	Cobb
Mississippi Delta Communities	~75	Low to Moderate	Hrdlička
South Carolina Gullah/Geechee	~73–74	Very Low	Ethnographic records

In other words, if you placed the skulls of Iron Age Judahites alongside those of modern African Americans, they'd match far more closely than they would with skulls from European-descended Jewish populations.

This isn't guesswork. It's math. And it corroborates everything else—the relief carvings, the skin textures, the hair types, the facial profiles.

The cephalic index becomes, in this case, a silent but powerful witness. One that confirms what the stones and sculptures have been saying all along.

Chapter 8

Reconsidering the Identity of the Biblical Israelites

So who were the Israelites—really?

The answer, buried beneath centuries of theological revision, colonial-era ethnography, and sanitized religious imagery, has been hiding in plain sight: carved into stone, sealed in ash, and etched into bone.

The Lachish Relief provides us with a visual dossier—etched by their enemies—of the ancient people of Judah: short, woolly hair, African facial features, and tightly curled, woolly beards. Their posture, their clothes, their faces—none of it resembles the European-styled depictions found in Sunday school illustrations or 20th-century cinema.

Then the bones speak. The cephalic index, skull dimensions, facial width, and cranial slope all match a profile not of modern Europeans or even most modern Middle Eastern populations—but of **Northeast Africans and African Americans**. In a contemporary context, if one were to reconstruct these people in a forensic lab, their appearance would draw comparison to people of color—not the white or olive-skinned populations often associated with biblical heritage.

They spoke Hebrew. They worshiped Yahuah. They were Semitic in language and custom—but in biology and physical expression, they were distinctly Afro-Asiatic. That's "Afro," which is short for African. Judah was not an isolated desert kingdom. It was a node in a vast cultural and genetic web stretching from Nubia to Canaan, from the Nile to the Jordan.

The archeological evidence reframes everything.

It challenges the conventional imagery of ancient Israelites. It complicates modern identity politics around the land of Israel. And it invites uncomfortable—but necessary—questions about historical erasure, forced displacement, and who has been written out of their own legacy.

So when Tucker Carlson asked, "Is the Israel of Genesis the same Israel run by Netanyahu today?"—the truthful answer is no. The land of the children of Israel of the Bible did and still does exist. However, its people looked more like your African American neighbor than a European-descended rabbi.

Figure 6.1. Lachish Captives. Photograph (left) by Alamy. Photograph (right) AI Generated, 8 Aug. 2025.

And that **truth**, once carved in stone and buried in silence, **has now been unearthed.**

Chapter 9

Was Jesus a Black Man?

Section 1: The Judah Connection — Following the Bloodline

If the people of Judah were undeniably African in appearance—as the Lachish Relief and associated skull studies suggest—then we must ask an explosive question:

What did Jesus look like?

This isn't a theological question. It's a forensic one. Jesus was born in Bethlehem of Judea. He was raised in Nazareth of Galilee. And according to the Gospels, he was known to his peers as a "son of David"—a direct descendant of the **tribe of Judah**.

In other words, **Jesus was a Judahite.**

That changes everything. Because if the archaeological record shows that the tribe of Judah, in the 7th century BCE, looked unmistakably African—woolly-haired, dolichocephalic, broad-featured—then we are forced to reexamine centuries of sanitized Christian iconography. The historical Jesus would not have resembled the blue-eyed, light-skinned figure so often portrayed in European churches and Renaissance paintings. He would have resembled the very men we saw kneeling in the Lachish Relief: **Black men.**

This isn't about political correctness. This is about historical continuity. Jesus' physical appearance cannot be divorced from his ethnic lineage—and his lineage traces back to a tribe that the ancient Assyrians depicted as African in appearance.

The logical question, then, is simple:

Do early depictions of Jesus match that African profile?

The answer—hidden in catacombs, lost frescoes, and obscure Christian manuscripts—might surprise you. Before the empire whitewashed the image of Jesus, it may have been something very different.

Section 2: The First Images of Jesus — Early Depictions Before Empire

Before Jesus was a symbol of power, he was a target of it. In the first few centuries after his death, Christians were hunted, jailed, and martyred by the Roman state. They worshipped underground, in catacombs and secret house churches. If they depicted Jesus at all, it wasn't for public display—it was for **survival**, for remembrance, and reverence. And in these rare, early images, we glimpse something that history nearly buried:

A Black Jesus.

The earliest surviving visual representations of Jesus are not found in the cathedrals of Europe, but in a forgotten church on the **Syrian frontier**, in a city buried by desert sand: **Dura-Europos**.

Discovered in the 1920s and dated to around **235 AD**, the Dura-Europos church is the oldest known Christian house of worship with preserved wall paintings. And in those paintings, we find **Jesus healing the paralytic**, walking on water, and standing among his disciples. But what's most striking is not

the narrative—it's the **face**.

He has **short hair, dark or olive skin, and in some frames, features that resemble those of Nubian or East African men**. He doesn't wear a golden halo or European robes. He looks like a **humble teacher**, dark-skinned and Middle Eastern in dress—almost indistinguishable from the everyday people of the region.

Figure 7.1. Photograph by Almay, The Healing of the Paralytic wall painting in the domus ecclesiae, Dura Europos.

These are not isolated impressions. **Other early Christian art**—including catacomb images in Rome and surviving Egyptian Coptic frescoes—presents Jesus without the flowing hair, pale skin, or noble Roman profile so common in later paintings. In these earliest moments, **Jesus resembles the people of that region**—and the people of that region were not white.

Figure 7.2. Coptic Picture of Christ. Cairo Museum, Cairo Egypt.

Question: So what changed?

Answer: By the 4th century, Christianity had been absorbed into imperial culture. The Jesus of the catacombs gave way to the Jesus of cathedrals. The once-persecuted Messiah was now the cosmic Christ of emperors—and his image was remodeled to fit their vision.

In the next section, we'll explore how the **Byzantine Empire transformed the face of Jesus**, replacing the woolly-haired Judean with a haloed Greco-Roman god. And how, in that transformation, **the memory of a Black Jesus began to fade—but never completely disappeared.**

Section 3: The Byzantine Makeover — From Black Messiah to Imperial Icon

By the early 4th century, everything changed.

What began as a grassroots faith preached by a dark-skinned teacher in Galilee was now the official religion of the Roman Empire. After Emperor Constantine's conversion in 312 AD, Christianity went from outlawed to honored—overnight. And with that shift came a powerful temptation: **to reshape Jesus into the image of the empire** that now served him.

—The Jesus of Dura-Europos—humble, brown-skinned, Middle Eastern—would not survive the makeover.

Figure 7.3. Christ treading the beasts, Museo Arcivescovile, Chapel of Saint Andrew, Ravenna, Italy.

In Byzantine art, a new image emerged: Jesus with **long flowing hair**, a **pale, oval face**, and **soft European features**. His clothing echoed the robes of Roman philosophers. His posture grew regal. His body slimmed and straightened. In the imperial mosaics of Ravenna and Constantinople, he no longer resembled the persecuted teacher from Judea. He resembled the **divine ruler** of a Greco-Roman cosmos.

Figure 7.4. Apsis mosaic, Santa Pudenziana, Rome.
This was no accident.

The Byzantines needed a **cosmic Christ**, one who legitimized their political power. And so Jesus became a king of kings—**not only in theology, but in art**. His skin lightened. His gaze lifted. His divinity swallowed his humanity. The gritty realism of the early church gave way to **gold-leaf halos and marble thrones**.

And yet, there's a chilling silence beneath all this splendor:

There are no surviving written descriptions of Jesus from the 1st to 3rd centuries—when his image might have still resembled the tribe of Judah depicted in the Lachish Relief.

Figure 7.5. The oldest known icon of Christ Pantocrator, a 6th-century encaustic icon from Saint Catherine's Monastery, Mount Sinai, South Sinai Governorate, Egypt.

By the time Christian scribes began copying the Gospels and the works of the Church Fathers on a broad scale, the image of Jesus had already undergone significant changes. The **earliest "descriptions" of Jesus** that survive today—like the **Letter of Lentulus**, which depicts him with golden hair and blue eyes— are known **forgeries** from the medieval period.

Figure 7.6. Christ in Majesty, Aberdeen Bestiary, 12th century AD.

What we have, then, is not silence by default—but **silence by design**.

While Western Christianity refined and reproduced the imperial Jesus for over a thousand years, **African, Nubian, and Coptic communities quietly held on to another face**—the one more closely aligned with the ancient people of Judah.

Section 4: Africa Remembers — The Survival of the Black Christ

While Europe reshaped Jesus to mirror Caesar, **Africa never forgot** what he truly looked like.

Across the deserts of Nubia, in the monasteries of Coptic Egypt, and high in the mountains of Ethiopia, early Christians preserved a **visual tradition** that stood in quiet resistance to the imperial makeover. Their Jesus looked nothing like a Roman emperor. He looked like them.

Figure 7.7. A painting of St. Mary in a window of the church of the same name on the shore of Lake Tana in northern Ethiopia.

In the ancient Christian kingdoms of **Nubia**—Nobatia, Makuria, and Alodia—Jesus was depicted on cathedral walls with **dark skin, curly hair, and African features**. These images, dated between the **7th and 14th centuries**, show Christ enthroned, flanked by angels, or offering blessings to African kings. They are bold, regal, and unmistakably Black.

Figure 7.8. Paintings of biblical scenes in rock-hewn church Petros and Paulus Melehayzengi, Tsaeda Amba mountains, Tigray, Ethiopia.

In **Ethiopia**, the story is even more striking. The **Garima Gospels**, dated between the **5th and 7th centuries**, are among the oldest surviving Christian manuscripts with illustrations. They show Jesus and his apostles with **brown to black skin**, rounded short-hair, and stylized African garments. Later wall paintings—especially in Lalibela and Tigray—continued this tradition well into the 19th century.

These aren't artistic anomalies. They are part of an **unbroken cultural memory**—a living tradition that honored Christ not

75

as a distant European monarch, but as a **member of their people**.

Even in **Coptic Egypt**, where Greco-Roman and Arab influences were strong, older images of Jesus still retained **Afro-Semitic traits**, including dark, almond-shaped eyes, thick, short hair, and deep brown skin.

All of this paints a powerful picture: while Rome was busy bleaching the image of Christ, **Africa was preserving the truth**.

These ancient communities—some of which had embraced Christianity before Europe ever heard the name—kept their eyes fixed on a Jesus who looked like **the men of Lachish**, like the people of Judah, like the poor and faithful who still suffer today.

Section 5: Hidden in the Vatican — The Black Jesus the Church Never Denied

While the Western world became saturated with pale-skinned portraits of Jesus, **the Roman Catholic Church quietly held on to something far older—and far darker**.

Tucked in the corners of European cathedrals, basilicas, and monasteries—often overlooked by tourists—are images of **Black Madonnas and Black Christs**, venerated for centuries by the faithful, yet seldom acknowledged by theologians or scholars. These aren't modern reinterpretations. Many date back to the **11th through 14th centuries**, and some even earlier.

One of the most famous is the **Black Madonna of Częstochowa** in Poland, a dark-skinned image of Mary and the infant Jesus, revered since the Middle Ages. Pilgrims have traveled to her shrine for centuries, praying not to a blonde Virgin, but to a woman of deep brown complexion holding a **Black child**—the Christ child.

Figure 7.9. The Jasna Góra Monastery (Luminous Mount), Czestochowa, Poland, The Famous Virgin Mary miraculous icon, High Altar.

In **Italy**, the sanctuary of **Our Lady of Montserrat** houses a statue of Mary and baby Jesus, both with African features and dark skin. The devotion is so fervent that this "La Moreneta" (the little Black one) is considered **patroness of Catalonia**.

And in **France**, at least **300 documented Black Madonnas** exist—carved, painted, and venerated—many of which **predate the Renaissance whitening of Jesus.** Some scholars suggest these statues preserved the memory of earlier African or Semitic imagery; others argue they reflected local peasant populations who identified with a darker-skinned holy family. Either way, the symbolism is unmistakable: **a Jesus of color was never entirely erased from the narrative.**

Even the **Vatican itself** holds paintings and sculptures from earlier eras depicting **a dark-skinned Christ**—some attributed to **Byzantine or Eastern Christian influence**, others to **African or Iberian traditions**. While these images have largely been pushed to the periphery of Church art, **they were never denounced or removed.**

Instead, they were **quietly absorbed**, kept in niches, chapels, and private devotional settings—while the official image of Christ became more European with each passing century.

In these images lies a subtle confession: that **the face of Christianity once looked different**, that its origins were darker, humbler, more human. And that somewhere beneath the gold and marble, the Church remembers.

Section 6: Why It Matters — The Psychology of a Whitewashed Messiah

Some might say it doesn't matter what Jesus looked like. That his color is irrelevant to his teachings. That his divinity transcends race.

And yet... the image of Jesus has shaped empires. It has adorned banners in crusades. It has stood in stained glass windows over slave plantations. It has been **weaponized, idealized, and globalized**—in the image of one people, at the expense of all others.

When the **Lamb of God is painted to look like Caesar**, the message is clear: **God looks like us—not you.**

This is not just art. It's psychology. A white Jesus has been used for centuries to justify power hierarchies, colonial dominance, and spiritual inferiority complexes. When millions of people—Black, Brown, Indigenous—are shown a savior who looks nothing like them, they are subtly told: holiness is whiteness. Divinity has a skin tone. And it isn't yours.

That's why this matters.

Because the evidence is there, the **Lachish Relief** shows the men of Judah—the tribe of Jesus—as unmistakably African. **The earliest images** of Jesus show a humble, brown-skinned healer. **The African church remembered him that way**, even after Europe forgot. And **the Catholic Church never entirely erased him**, only replaced him in plain sight.

Conclusion

The question **"Was Jesus a Black man?"** isn't rhetorical. It's archaeological. It's artistic. It's genetic. It's spiritual.

And if the answer is yes—and the evidence says it is—then the implications are profound. Because it means the world's most recognized religious figure has been culturally hijacked, his face repainted to serve kings and empires rather than truth.

It means that many of the most oppressed people in history—enslaved, colonized, erased—were closer in appearance to the Son of God than those who claimed to own his legacy.

It means we need to **unlearn and relearn**, not just the facts, but the story. The face. The truth.

Jesus was a man of Judah. The men of Judah looked like Africans. The earliest Christians knew this. The oldest images showed this. And the oldest bones confirm it.

Figure 8.1. Photograph by Almay. Lachish Captives.

We've only just begun to uncover what was buried...

Illustration Credits

Chapter 1

Figure 1.1 - Matson Collection, Public domain, via Wikimedia Commons.

Chapter 3

Figure 3.1 – Photograph by Alamy - Assyrian Lion Hunt. The Capture of Lachish. Jan. 2015. British Museum, London, England UK.

Figure 3.2 – Photography by Alamy - Sennacherib watches the capture of Lachish. Sennacherib, on a throne, watches as prisoners are brought before him and sometimes executed. Assyrian relief. about 700-692 BC. Nineveh, South-West Palace, Room XXXVI, panela 11-13.

Figure 3.3 – Photograph by Alamy - Cuneiform inscription from Lachish Relief.

Figure 3.4 – Photograph by Alamy - Scene from the Lachish' Relief depicting the defeated inhabitants begging for their lives. Relief from Sennacherib's palace.

Chapter 4

Figure 4.1 – Photograph by Alamy - A detail of an ancient Assyrian stone panel carving (700-692BC) showing archers attacking the town of Lachish near Jerusalem. British Museum. 11th Apr. 2018, London, England.

Figure 4.2 - Stone carved relief depicting an attack on Lachish, Assyria. about 700-692 BC. Nineveh, South-West Palace.

Figure 4.3 - Photograph by Alamy - Scene from the Lachish Relief depicting the defeated inhabitants begging for their lives. Relief from Sennacherib's palace.

Figure 4.4 - The Fall of Lachish: King Sennacherib reviews Judaean prisoners. Shadsluiter, CC BY-SA 4.0 <https://creativecommons.org/licenses/by-sa/4.0>, via Wikimedia Commons.

Figure 4.5 – Photograph by Alamy - Stone carved relief depicting prisoners captured after the attack on Lachish, Assyria. about 700-692 BC.

Figure 4.6 - Assyrian soldier, using a dagger, about to behead a prisoner from the city of Lachish. South-West Palace, Nineveh, Mesopotamia. British Museum. Shadsluiter, CC BY-SA 4.0 <https://creativecommons.org/licenses/by-sa/4.0>, via Wikimedia Commons.

Figure 4.7 - The captives are brought before King Sennacherib. Shadsluiter, CC BY-SA 4.0 <https://creativecommons.org/licenses/by-sa/4.0>, via Wikimedia Commons.

Chapter 5

Figure 5.1. The captives are brought before King Sennacherib.

Figure 5.2 Ethiopian.

Figure 5.3. Barbados copper penny coin minted in 1792.

Figure 5.4 AI Image.

Figure 5.5 Moors.

Figure 5.6 Nubians wearing hair wigs

Figure 5.7 Nubians.

Figure 5.8 Egyptian soldiers and Nubian mercenaries around 1470 BC Deir el-Bahri, the mortuary temple of Queen, Hatshepsut.

Figure 5.9 Nubian.

Figure 9.1 – Photograph by Alamy - The Healing of the Paralytic: wall painting in the baptistry of the domus ecclesiae. Dura Europos.

Figure 9.2 – Coptic Picture of Christ in the Cairo Museum. Public Domain.

Figure 9.3 – Christ treading the beasts. Chapel of Saint Andrew. Português: Museo Arcivescovile. Ravenna, Italy. Wikipedia.

Figure 9.4 - Apsis mosaic. Santa Pudenziana, Rome. Wikipedia.

Figure 9.5 – The oldest known icon of Christ Pantocrator, 6th-century encaustic icon from Saint Catherine's Monastery. Mount Sinai. Wikipedia.

Figure 9.6 – Christ in Majesty. Folio 4 verso from the Aberdeen Bestiary. University of Aberdeen Library. Public Domain via Wikimedia Commons.

Figure 9.7 – Photograph by iStock Photo - A painting of St Mary in a window of the church of the same name on the shore of Lake Tana, Northern Ethiopia.

Figure 9.8 – Photograph by Alamy - Paintings of biblical scenes in rock-hewn church Petros and Paulus Melehayzengi. Tsaeda Amba mountains, Tigray, Ethiopia.

Figure 9.10 – Photo Alamy Photo - The Jasna Góra Monastery (Luminous Mount), The Famous Virgin Mary miraculous icon, High Altar. Poland, Czestochowa.

Conclusion

Figure 10.1 – Alamy Photo – Lachish Judah Captives.

Who Are the Biblical Israelites?